To:

_____

May you be blessed
by the LORD,
the Maker of
heaven and earth.

PSALM 115:15

From:

Aunt Kelly &
Uncle Greg

Compiler: Emily Klotz
Associate Editor: Molly Detweiler
Designer: Chris Gannon
Illustrations: Karen Clark

Printed in China
00 01 02 /HK/ 5 4 3 2 1

Little Ones To Him Belong

inspirio

The gift group of Zondervan

All This And More

God made the sunlight, but it cannot laugh,
God made the moonbeams, but they cannot smile;
God made the stars, but they cannot play;
God made the birds, but they cannot hold the heart;
God made music, but it cannot love.
So, God made you, my child.

DORCAS S. MILLER

"Before I formed you in the womb I knew you,
before you were born I set you apart,"
says the LORD.

JEREMIAH 1:5

Jesus said, "Whoever welcomes one of these little children in my name welcomes me; and whoever welcomes me does not welcome me but the one who sent me."

MARK 9:37

God, help us prepare our children for the arrival of this new life. Make us sensitive to all of our children's needs. Give us wisdom as we encourage our children to love and appreciate each other.

GENE & LISA FANT

Little children, little children
Who love their Redeemer
Are the jewels, precious jewels,
His loved and his own;
Like the stars of the morning,
his bright crown adorning,
They shall shine in their beauty—
Bright gems for his crown.

WILLIAM O. CUSHING

Jesus said,
"Let the little children come to me,
and do not hinder them, for the kingdom
of heaven belongs to such as these."

MATTHEW 19:14

What is a Baby?

A baby is a soft little hand,
curling warmly around your finger.
A baby is a lively little pair of legs,
kicking happily in the air after a bath.
A baby is a puckered and trembling lower lip,
trying hard, oh so hard, to tell you something.
A baby is a cry in the night,
calling you swiftly out of sleep and to its crib.

A baby is an eloquent pair of eyes,
one time dancing with glee …
another time staring at you with sober reflection.
But above all a baby is a priceless gift from God.
Those little hands must learn to move in his service;
those little feet must grow up to walk in his ways;
and those little eyes must learn to focus on his Word.

AUTHOR UNKNOWN

The Lord will not let your foot slip—
he who watches over you will not slumber.
PSALM 121:3

Our sons in their youth will be like well-nutured
plants, and our daughters will be like pillars
carved to adorn a palace. ...
Blessed are the people whose God is the Lord.
PSALM 144:12, 15

The Lord will keep you from all harm—
he will watch over your life;
the Lord will watch over your coming and going
both now and forevermore.
PSALM 121:7–8

Where Did You Come From, Baby Dear?

Where did you come from, baby dear?
Out of the everywhere into here.
Where did you get your eyes so blue?
Out of the sky as I came through.
Where did you get this pearly ear?
God spoke, and it came out to hear.
But how did you come to us, you dear?
God thought about you, and so I am here.

GEORGE MACDONALD

God, thank you for watching over our little ones as they grow. Help us to remember their miraculous status as creations in the image of God.

GENE & LISA FANT

For you created my inmost being, O Lord;
you knit me together in my mother's womb.
I praise you because I am fearfully and wonderfully
made; your works are wonderful, I know that full well.
My frame was not hidden from you
when I was made in the secret place.
When I was woven together in the depths of the
earth, your eyes saw my unformed body. All the days
ordained for me were written in your book before
one of them came to be.

PSALM 139:13-16

God will silently plan for you some
wonderful surprise of love.
No eye has seen no ear has heard,
but it is kept for you above.
He will silently plan for you,
happy child of a Father's care,
As if no other claimed His love,
but you alone to Him were dear.

E. MARY GRIMES

Dear Lord, ... help [my baby] to grow up pliable to [your] will, Lord, responsive to every touch of your hand upon her life. Shape within her a spirit so sensitive to spiritual things that she will be able to feel your breath when you whisper to her conscience, sense your shadow when you move across the circumstances of her life.

Use this little life to mold me, Lord. Use her clinging fingers to make me more gentle and her sudden smile to make me more joyful. Use her countless spills to make me more patient and her helpless cries to make me more compassionate. Use her to mold me not only into more of a mother but more of a human being.

MARY C. AND ROBERT G. WELLS,
JUDY AND KEN GIRE

I see the sunshine in your smile.

You mean so much, my precious child.
I'm here to help you learn and grow,
And share with you the things I know.
But most of all I hope that you
Will love God 'cause he loves you too.

AUTHOR UNKNOWN

I give to you a golden thread of love and hope
and faith. Its strength can never be broken,
for it was made in heaven, nurtured through the ages,
and designed to be yours forever.

FLAVIA AND LISA WEEDN

What a joy and precious gem you are, my child!

A gift from God I've just barely begun to open.

Every good and perfect gift is from above, coming down from the Father of the heavenly lights, who does not change like shifting shadows.

JAMES 1:17

What a wonder you've made, God!

Eyes that can see the unseen.

Ears that can hear innermost thoughts.

A mouth that can bestow blessings or swallow hurts

before they have injured another.

Hands that can carry immeasurable burdens.

A heart that can beat with divine love.

A mind that can believe and learn and grow.

What a wonder you've made! What a wonder I am!

FRANCIS THOMPSON

The great events of this world are not battles
and earthquakes and hurricanes.
The great events of this world are babies.

Sons are a heritage from the Lord,
children a reward from him.

<small>Psalm 127:3</small>

The moon shines bright,

The stars give light

Before the break of day;

God bless you all

Both great and small

And send you a joyful day.

TRADITIONAL

When Father Prays

When Father prays he doesn't use
The words the preacher does;
There's different things for different days,
But mostly it's for us.

When Father prays the house is still,
His voice is low and deep.
We shut our eyes, the clock ticks loud,
So quiet we must keep.

He prays that we may be good boys,
And later on good men;
And then we squirm, and think we won't
Have any quarrels again.

You'd never think, to look at Dad,
He once had tempers, too.
I guess if Father needs to pray,
We youngsters surely do.

Sometimes the prayer gets very long
And hard to understand,
And then I wiggle up quite close,
And let him hold my hand.

I can't remember all of it,
I'm little yet, you see;
But one thing I cannot forget,
My father prays for me!

AUTHOR UNKNOWN

Children hold the gift of innocence.
When we open our eyes to their
wisdom, we find the wondrous
simplicity of life's beauty.

FLAVIA AND LISA WEEDN

This is my prayer: that your love may
abound more and more in knowledge
and depth of insight, so that you may
be able to discern what is best and
may be pure and blameless until the
day of Christ.

PHILIPPIANS 1:9–10

Baby Shoes

Often tiny baby feet,
Tired from their play,
Kick off scuffed-up little shoes
At the close of day.
And often tired mothers
Find them lying there,
And over them send up to God
This fervent, whispered prayer:
God guide their every footstep
In paths where thou hast stood;
God, make them brave; God, make
them strong;
And please, God, make them good!

MARY HOLMES

Before you came, I knew that I would love you.
I knew that there was room in my heart for you.
But I thought that it would take time for us to
bond; that my love for you would grow a
little each day. After all, that's how love
is supposed to happen. What a surprise!
They brought you to me for the very first time.
As I held you and looked into the haze of your
newborn eyes, I knew that I had been wrong.
My love for you is complete.

PATRICIA SPRINKLE

As a father has compassion on his children,
so the LORD has compassion on
those who fear him.

PSALM 103:13

Come, my children, listen to me;
I will teach you the fear of the LORD.

PSALM 34:11

He who fears the LORD has a secure fortress,
and for his children it will be a refuge.

PROVERBS 14:26

My Little Boy

Dear Lord, I want this little boy to know how much I love him. I want him to know how much joy he has brought to my life. I realize, Lord, that he won't understand these things, at least not fully, until someday when he has children of his own. But Lord, help him even now to understand this: Help him to know how much he is wanted. ...

May his childhood be filled with such happy times, Lord, that when he looks back on them, twenty, thirty, forty years hence, the memories will bring a smile to his face and a reassurance that he was wanted, and that he was loved.

MARY C. AND ROBERT G. WELLS, JUDY AND KEN GIRE

A Childlike Heart

Children really are good at open-
hearted, spontaneous joy. They know
it intuitively. That's why they use it
lavishly in the present moment.
They don't put it in a savings account
for a rainy day. They don't put it on
hold or put a lid on it.
They spend it with abandon.
They practice it at every small
occasion. That's why they are such
pros at getting it right!

CLAIRE CLONINGER

From the lips of children and infants
you have ordained praise, O Lord. ...

PSALM 8:2

Our children are the mothers
and fathers of tomorrow.
Let their lives be written with
grace and gentle kindnesses.

I was young and now I am old,
yet I have never seen the righteous forsaken
or their children begging bread.
They are always generous and lend freely;
their children will be blessed.

PSALM 37:25–26

He who gives a child a treat
Makes joy-bells ring in Heaven's street,
And he who gives a child a home
Builds palaces in Kingdom come,
And she who gives a baby birth
Brings Savior Christ again to Earth,
For life is joy, and mind is fruit,
And body's precious earth and root.

JOHN MASEFIELD

Jesus said,

"See that you do not look down on one of these little ones. For I tell you that their angels in heaven always see the face of my Father in heaven."

MATTHEW 18:10

The Way of Angels

When I'm afraid for my children, my first
impulse is to run to You. All our hopes are in
Your hands. ... Thank you for Your angels of
mercy and power who guard even the weakest in
your kingdom. ... Lord, I choose to accept the
risks of living, knowing that my children are held
in Your strong embrace for all eternity.
Amen.

DAVID & HEATHER KOPP

The Lord will command his angels concerning
you to guard you in all your ways;
they will lift you up in their hands, so that you
will not strike your foot against a stone.

PSALM 91:11–12

28

Lullaby Town

There's a quaint little place they call
Lullaby Town—

It's just back of those hills where the
sunsets go down.

Its streets are of silver,
its buildings of gold,
And its palaces dazzling
things to behold;

There are dozens of spires,
housing musical chimes;
Its people are folk from the
Nursery Rhymes,

And at night it's alight,
like a garden of gleams,
With angels, who bring the
most wonderful dreams.

JOHN IRVING DILLER

Childhood, whose very happiness is love.

LETITIA ELIZABETH LANDON

Jesus said, "If anyone gives even a cup of cold water to one of these little ones because he is my disciple, I tell you the truth, he will certainly not lose his reward."

MATTHEW 10:42

I am always with you, Lord;
you hold me by my right hand.

PSALM 73:23

I remember thinking, lying there next to this baby person, *I'll be your daddy, little girl. You can count on me. I can do this. I know I can. God, please help me.*

ROBERT WOLGEMUTH

One laugh of a child will make the holiest day more sacred still.

R.G. INGERSOLL

Yesterday you were only a word: Baby. Only a ripple within me, a dream, a hope. Now today you are YOU: someone with a name, a face, a personality of your very own. Today you are someone I talk to.
A Bible phrase comes to mind:
"the Word became flesh."
You become very holy to me, Child,
when I realize that when God wanted to show
exactly what he was like, he sent a baby.

PATRICIA SPRINKLE

Sharing a quiet moment with my baby is like heaven on earth to me. Smelling the clean, soft skin of a newborn, listening to the deep, gentle breathing of a peaceful slumber. … What more is there to life than this kind of silent pleasure?

From birth I have relied on you;
   you brought me forth from my
   mother's womb, O Lord.
   I will ever praise you.

PSALM 71:6

Cradle Song

Sweet babe, in thy face

Soft desires I can trace,

Secret joys and secret smiles,

Little pretty infant wiles.

As thy softest limbs I feel

Smiles as of the morning steal

O'er thy cheek, and o'er thy breast

Where thy little heart doth rest.

WILLIAM BLAKE

A Mother's Prayer

Lord, give me patience when wee hands
Tug at me with their small demands.
Give me gentle and smiling eyes;
Keep my lips from hasty replies.
Let not weariness, confusion, or noise
Obscure my vision of life's fleeting joys.

BRENDA AND JOHN WARD

May your father and mother be glad;
may she who gave you birth rejoice!

PROVERBS 23:25

Few things are more
tender than a baby,
Unless, of course,
we count the hearts
of the mothers who
have just looked on that
baby for the first time.

BRENDA AND JOHN WARD

The Lord will love you and bless you and increase
your numbers. He will bless the fruit of your womb.

DEUTERONOMY 7:13

The Lord your God is with you,
he is mighty to save.
He will take great delight in you,
he will quiet you with his love,
he will rejoice over you with singing.

ZEPHANIAH 3:17

May God give you the desire of your heart
and make all your plans succeed.
Psalm 20:4

Day is done,

Gone the sun,

From the lake, from the hills,

from the sky.

All is well, safely rest,

God is nigh.

How did you come to me, my sweet?

From the land that no man knows?
Did Mr. Stork bring you here on his wings?
Were you born in the heart of a rose?

Did an angel fly with you down from the sky?
Were you found in a gooseberry patch?
Did a fairy bring you from fairyland
To my door—that was left on a latch?

No—my darling was born of a wonderful love,
A love that was Daddy's and mine.
A love that was human, but deep and profound,
A love that was almost divine.

OLGA PETROVA

In the course of time Hannah conceived
and gave birth to a son. She named him Samuel,
saying, "Because I asked the LORD for him."

1 SAMUEL 1:20

For such a child I bless God, in whose bosom he is!
May I and mine become as this little child.

JOHN EVELYN

You, my precious little one, complete me.
You are the finest part of me, and
because of you I know why I am
here and where I belong.

FLAVIA AND LISA WEEDN

I think God gives the children,
as through the land they go,
The most delightful mission
that anyone can know.
He wants us to be sunbeams of love
and hope and cheer,
To brighten up the shadows that
often gather here.

O we are little sunbeams,
sent down from God to man;
In all life's shady places,
we shine as best we can.

EBEN EUGENE REXFORD

Gentle Jesus, meek and mild,
Look upon a little child,
Pity my simplicity,
Suffer me to come to Thee.

CHARLES WESLEY

As you lie on your blanket, waving your hands and feet and trying to understand your fingers and toes, you give me such pleasure! You gurgle deep in your throat and then light up with such a wide, toothless grin that I have to grin too. I touch your cheek, ruffle your fuzzy hair, and love you so much it makes me shiver.

PATRICIA SPRINKLE

Dear God, may my child learn to love you with all her heart, and with all her soul and with all her mind (Matthew 22:37).

ELISA MORGAN

We need love's tender lessons taught
As only weakness can;
God hath made His small interpreters;
The child must teach the man.

JOHN GREENLEAF WHITTIER

Blessed are the pure in heart, for they will see God.

MATTHEW 5:8

I love to watch you at play, little child.
Your bright smile and squint-eyed chuckle
make me forget all my anxieties.
The Lord has blessed me immeasureably
with your playfulness, and has taught me
how to have childlike fun again.

May the righteous be glad
and rejoice before God;
may they be happy and joyful.

PSALM 68:3

Children think not of what is past,
not what is to come,
but enjoy the present time, which few of us do.

LA BRUYERE

The soul is healed
by being with children.

FYODOR DOSTOEVSKY

Women know

The way to rear up children (to be just),
They know a simple, merry, tender knack
Of tying sashes, fitting baby-shoes,
And stringing pretty words that make no sense,
And kissing full sense into empty words.

ELIZABETH BARRETT BROWNING

i've been waiting for you now
no more wondering about me—
whether or not this miracle of life will happen inside me

now I can wonder about you—
about what color threads
He's weaving you with

brown eyes or blue
will you like to swim or draw
bake bread or engineer buildings
will you throw your head back
and laugh hard
or just grin

i don't know
i don't know

but I do know that I will love to hear you call my name
i will love to feel your tiny hand in mine
i will love to watch your tummy
rise and fall
in sweet sleep ...

but until then
please baby grow strong
take all you can from me please

until then
I'll be waiting for you

JULIE MARTIN

Before becoming a mother I had a hundred
theories on how to bring up children.
Now I have seven children and only one theory:
love them, especially when they
least deserve to be loved.

KATE SAMPERI

We wait in hope for the Lord;
he is our help and our shield.
In him our hearts rejoice,
for we trust in his holy name.
May your unfailing love rest upon us,
O Lord, even as we put our hope in you.

PSALM 33:20–22

We must remember not to let our quest for the best get in the way of our relationship with our children. Sometimes the best thing is to put down the work and pick up the child.

BRENDA AND JOHN WARD

Oh, cleaning and scrubbing
will wait till tomorrow,
But children grow up,
As I've learned to my sorrow.
So quiet down cobwebs.
Dust, go to sleep.
I'm rocking my baby
Babies don't keep.

RUTH HULBERT HAMILTON

A child's hand in yours—
what tenderness and power it arouses.
You are instantly the very touchstone
of wisdom and strength.

MARJORIE HOLMES

The wolf will live with the lamb,
the leopard will lie down with the
goat, the calf and the lion and the
yearling together;
and a little child will lead them.

ISAIAH 11:6

little love
tiny toes
mama's eyes
daddy's nose

beautiful baby
pure, smooth skin
please won't you stay
innocent within?

There are only two lasting bequests
we can hope to give our children.
One is roots; the other, wings.

HODDING CARTER

Those who hope in the LORD
will renew their strength.
They will soar on wings like eagles;
they will run and not grow weary,
they will walk and not be faint.

ISAIAH 40:31

The sonogram. We are about to snatch a
glimpse of the miracle of life. Do we dare?
Lying on the cool vinyl table,
I look over my shoulder at the black screen.
The doctor flips on the switch. An image appears.
And I wonder if God allowed the angels to watch
Him form Adam from the dust.

JULIE MARTIN

Slow down,
You grow up too fast;
Keep my fingers forever
Wrapped in your tiny fist.

Dear God, convince my child that she can do everything through you, who give her strength (Philippians 4:13).

ELISA MORGAN

The child grew and became strong;
he was filled with wisdom,
and the grace of God was upon him.

LUKE 2:40

A new baby is like the beginning of all things—
wonder, hope, a dream of possibilities.

EDA J. LESHAN

My Child

It was a night I won't forget
When you came into my life;
A miracle was right before my eyes.
This little baby girl
Would steal my heart away,
And I was left with just one thing to say …

You are my child,
A precious one;
You are a miracle of God's unending love.
You are my child,
And now it's plain to see
How great a love the Father has for me.

As I lay you down to sleep
With the angels at your side,
I pray that you would give your heart away
To the One who chose to die,
Who loved you with his life.
And just for you He'd do it all again.

You are my child,
A precious one;
You are a miracle of God's unending love.
You are my child,
And now it's plain to see
How great a love the Father has for me.

DAN KLOTZ

Jesus ... took a little child and had him stand beside him. Then he said to [his disciples], "Whoever welcomes this little child in my name welcomes me; and whoever welcomes me welcomes the one who sent me. For he who is least among you all—he is the greatest."

LUKE 9:47-48

Like the first flower in Spring, you are welcome and loved.

We are God's workmanship, created in Christ Jesus to do good works.

EPHESIANS 2:10

Today, for the first time,

I realize that you and I are separate, and the thought makes me a little afraid. I know, of course, that you have been a separate person for a long time, even when you were cradled within me, but I have grown so accustomed to thinking of you as a part of me. Today I realize that one day you will grow up—and away.

As you grow, you will see, hear, and believe things that are not what I see, hear or believe. You may like things that I dislike, and dislike some things that I love. God and you together may even choose for you a purpose, a path, that is not at all what I would have chosen for you. …

I pray, … Little One, that whatever path you take, you will walk with God.

PATRICIA SPRINKLE

I kiss your chilly hands and that
little rounded forehead.
I squeeze your chubby cheeks
and legs. You giggle and grab my
nose. These are the moments that
will last forever in my memory—
Or at least until the next really
cute thing you do.

God has brought me laughter. ...
GENESIS 21:6

I love these little people;
and it is not a slight thing when they,
who are so fresh from God, love us.

CHARLES DICKENS

Be imitators of God, therefore,
as dearly loved children
and live a life of love.

EPHESIANS 5:1-2

Children are the keys of Paradise.

R. H. STODDARD

All night, all day,
Angels watching over me, my Lord.
All night, all day,
Angels watching over me.

Sun is a-setting in the West;
Angels watching over me, my Lord.
Sleep my child, take your rest;
Angels watching over me.

All night, all day,
Angels watching over me, my Lord.
All night, all day,
Angels watching over me.

TRADITIONAL AMERICAN FOLK SONG

If you make children happy now, you will make them happy twenty years hence when they think of it.

KATE DOUGLAS WIGGIN

Happy is he that is happy in his children.

THOMAS FULLER

As you grow and change, some things will stay the same. I'll always love you. I'll always hug you. I'll always be on your side. And I want you to know that ... just in case you ever wonder.

MAX LUCADO

Baby Face

Baby face, you've got the
cutest little baby face
There's not another one
could take your place
Baby face, my poor heart is jumpin;
You sure have started somethin'
Baby face, I'm up in heaven
When I'm in your fond embrace,
I didn't need a shove
'Cause I just fell in love
With your pretty baby face.

BENNIE DAVIS AND HARRY AKST

In praise of little children

I will say God first made man,
then found a better way for woman,
but his third way was the best.
Of all created things the loveliest
And most divine are children.

WILLIAM CANTON

We all want to be good moms.

You can best meet your child's needs by
keeping your focus on the main thing
in mothering: loving your child.
The rest will eventually fall into place.

ELISA MORGAN AND CAROL KUYKENDALL

The Lord tends his flock like a shepherd: He gathers the lambs in his arms and carries them close to his heart; He gently leads those that have young.

ISAIAH 40:11

If there is anything that will endure
The eye of God, because it still is pure,
It is the spirit of a little child,
Fresh from his hand, and therefore undefiled.

R.H. STODDARD

Thank you for children brought into being because we loved. God of love, keep us loving so that they may grow up whole in love's overflow.

JOE BAYLY

Father God, help me be a successful parent
(Your definition of success means
relying completely on You),
and to take advantage of the precious
years of my child's early life.
Help me enjoy him while he is little
so he knows how much he means to me
even when he is grown.

"As a mother comforts her child,
so I will comfort you," says the Lord.

ISAIAH 66:13

Little Lamb, who made thee?
Dost thou know who made thee?
Gave thee life and beg thee feed
By the stream and o'er the mead;
Gave thee clothing of delight,
Softest clothing, woolly, bright.

Little Lamb, I'll tell thee,
Little Lamb I'll tell thee:
He is called by thy name
For he calls himself a Lamb.
He is meek and he is mild;
He became a little child.
I a child, and thou a lamb,
We are called by his name.
Little Lamb, God bless thee!
Little Lamb, God bless thee!

WILLIAM BLAKE

Dear Lord,

I plead for my children that they will grow every day in wisdom and good reputation as You did (Luke 2:52). Help me to do my part to raise them to be wise adults, able to make right choices that will bring each one a life-time of blessing—and bring You glory!

May my children always remember that knowing you personally is the best human knowledge of all.
Amen.

DAVID AND HEATHER KOPP

If a child is to keep alive this
inborn sense of wonder …
he needs the companionship of at least
one adult who can share it,
rediscovering with him the joy,
excitement and mystery
of the world we live in.

RACHEL CARLSON

My son, if your heart is wise,
then my heart will be glad;
my inmost being will rejoice
when your lips speak what is right.

PROVERBS 23:15

"The fruit of your womb will be blessed," says the Lord. ...

DEUTERONOMY 28:4

When the voices of children
are heard on the green
And laughing is heard on the hill,
My heart is at rest within my breast
And everything else is still.

WILLIAM BLAKE

Jesus, Faithful Shepherd,

Thank You that You know each of us so well
You call us by name (John 10:3).
Today I lift the names of my children to You,
and I praise You for each little lamb
you've given me.

DAVID AND HEATHER KOPP

Flesh of their flesh protects the home from
separation. Surely there should be other
reasons for togetherness, but children do
tend to unify the parents. Drawn together
by an object of mutual love and held by two
tiny hands, one in the hand of the mother,
and the other in the hand of the father, they
renew their commitment to each other.

FROM *A PSALM IN MY HEART*

Tell me the stories of Jesus I love to hear;
Things I would ask Him to tell me if He were here;
Scenes by the wayside, tales of the sea,
Stories of Jesus, tell them to me.

First let me hear how the
children stood round His knee,
And I shall fancy His blessing resting on me;
Words full of kindness, deeds full of grace,
All in the love light of Jesus' face.

WILLIAM HENRY PARKER

When Simeon and Anna discovered they would see their Savior face-to-face, they spent their days rejoicing and worshiping God, right up until the day when Joseph and Mary brought Jesus to temple for his dedication. Their hopeful expectation was great, but not as great as the joy they felt on that day. We feel that same expectation regarding our baby. As we think about the joy over its coming, we are reminded about the even greater joy we should have in knowing that the Christ child has already come and has brought salvation into the world. Now we understand even better the joyous expectation that accompanied Christ's birth.

God, we thank you for the birth of our Savior, and we thank you for the expectation we now have over the birth of our child. Make us patient as we wait, and make us joyous in our expectation.

GENE AND LISA FANT

we are your everything
when your daddy cut the cord
it was only a beginning of dependency
for from our hearts you will take all you need
and the best we can give you is Jesus.

the best we can show you is His love
so that one day all you need
will come from His heart and
He will be your everything.

JULIE MARTIN

Prince of Peace,

Today I pray that my children might be
peacemakers and sons of God (Matthew 5:9).
I pray that they would know Your
peace that passes all understanding (Philippians 4:7).
And as a result that their peaceable
love would overflow to others (1 Thessalonians 3:12).
… Show me how, day by day, to raise children to cher-
ish unity and harmony in Your kingdom.
In Jesus' name.
Amen.

DAVID AND HEATHER KOPP

A Little Child

Give me a little child to point the way
Over the strange, sweet path that leads to thee;
Give me a little voice to teach to pray;
Give me two shining eyes thy face to see.
The only crown I ask, dear Lord, to wear
Is this: that I may teach a little child.

AUTHOR UNKNOWN

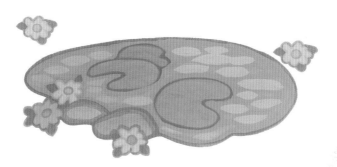

A Prayer for You

May you always be aware of the beauty around you even in the seemingly mundane events of life. May you be blessed with family and teachers who allow you to express yourself and help guide you in your special talents. And may you grow into the knowledge that you are God's child, always surrounded by his love, his care, and his peace.

Amen.

Dear Baby,

I find myself wondering for the millionth time how anyone could be so beautiful, so perfect. Everything about you seems miraculous to me; every motion, every sound is significant. Nothing you do is too small to be wondrous.

Many, O Lord my God,
are the wonders you have done.
The things you planned for us
no one can recount to you;
were I to speak and tell of them,
they would be too many to declare.

PSALM 40:5

God has blessed you,

my child, with time. Use it wisely.
If you take time to work, you will find success;
take time to play, you will stay young;
take time to read, wisdom will be yours;
take time for friends, you will be happy;
take time to worship, you will find strength;
but take time to love and be loved,
and you will find God.

Dear God, remind my child
that you made her the way she is.
You knit her together into a child that is fearfully
and wonderfully made.
Amen.

You brought me out of the womb,
O Lord; you made me trust in you
even at my mother's breast.

PSALM 22:9

As you grow, my child,

you will need to make three choices: who will be your master, what will be your mission, and who will be your mate. Make worthy choices, but take no chances. God's guidance will be true each time.

ANONYMOUS

Dear little lips with the happy smile,
Making home beautiful all the while,
Speak only true, loving words today,
Try to please Jesus in all you say.

Jesus wants me to be loving,
And kind to all I see;
Showing how pleasant and happy
His little one can be.

A sunbeam, a sunbeam,
Jesus wants me for a sunbeam;
A sunbeam, a sunbeam,
I'll be a sunbeam for Him.

NELLIE TALBOT

To love your child unconditionally is to determine that no matter what, you will always seek his or her highest good, not your own.

The righteous man leads a blameless life;
blessed are his children after him.

PROVERBS 20:7

Jesus loves me! This I know,
For the Bible tells me so.
Little ones to Him belong;
They are weak, but He is strong.

Yes, Jesus loves me!
Yes, Jesus loves me!
Yes, Jesus loves me!
The Bible tells me so.

ANNA BARTLETT WARNER

As we watch you smile
and watch you grow,
Our job is to train you
how you should go.
What a joy you are
every day.
God bless you now
and always.

CONOVER

Children's children are a crown to the aged,
and parents are the pride of their children.

PROVERBS 17:6

In teaching our children about God's righteous-
ness, we will be laying the path for our children
to do the same, and for their children as well.
We will be playing a part in the training of future
generations of believers who will worship God.
We hope someday to be the grandparents of little girls and boys who will receive a spiritual
inheritance from us.

GENE AND LISA FANT

O Lord of my nights,

Your delight in my family is all around

me, even at night. We're healthy, safe,

warm, and fed. You've surrounded my

children with a world of small beauties

and large mysteries. ...

At bedtime or during the night when

those quiet moments come, help me to

lead each of my children in his or her

own expression of love to You. During

those moments turn our thoughts away

from our little troubles. ... May I sing

new songs of joy to You,

Lord of my nights!

Amen.

DAVID AND HEATHER KOPP

A Gift from God

You are a blessing in our life;

we asked the Lord for you;

Yes, babies are a gift from God;

The Bible says that's true.

He gave us a most wondrous gift

To love our whole lives through;

And so we thank God every day

For the precious gift of you.

CONOVER

A Prayer for Bathtime

I wash the dirt from off two feet,
and as I wash I pray,
Lord, keep them ever pure and true
to walk the narrow way.
I wash the dirt from little hands,
and earnestly I ask,
Lord, may they ever yielded be
to do the humblest task.
I wash the dirt from soiled knees,
and pray, Lord, may they be
The place where victories are won,
and orders sought from thee.

B. RYBERG

All your sons will be taught by the LORD,
and great will be your children's peace.

ISAIAH 54:13

I am the LORD your God,
who teaches you what is best for you,
who directs you in the way you should go.

ISAIAH 48:17

The LORD is good and his
love endures forever;
his faithfulness continues
through all generations.

PSALM 100:5

A Child's Daily Prayer

Guide my hands, guide my feet;
May my words be ever sweet.
Keep a watch on what I see;
Hold me ever close to thee.
And I'll thank you every day
For your blessings when I pray.
Amen.

SARAH MICHAELS

It is God who made us, and we are his;
we are his people,
the sheep of his pasture.

PSALM 100:3

Lord,

You are my child's Shepherd.
Because her care is Your personal
concern, she will never be without
anything she truly needs. (PSALM 23:1)

Yes, Lord, may Your unfailing
goodness and tender mercies sur-
round her all the days of her life,
and may she find her true home in
Your presence forever. (PSALM 23:6)

Amen.

DAVID AND HEATHER KOPP

Jesus' little flock are we;
Where He is, we want to be;
He's our Shepherd kind and dear;
Now His loving call we hear.

Dear God, speak to my child in his heart.
Imprint your voice on his memory that
he may learn to discern your voice
from the voices of others.
Amen.

Jesus is the Shepherd true,

And He'll always stand by you,

For He loves the little children of the world;

He's a Savior great and strong,

And He'll shield you from the wrong,

For He loves the little children of the world.

C. HERBERT WOOLSTON

Dear God, develop habits of prayer, honesty and hard work in my child while he is young so that when he is older, he will enjoy their contribution to his life.

ELISA MORGAN

Save your people and bless your inheritance, O Lord; be their shepherd and carry them forever.

PSALM 28:9

Child, I give you a blessing of prayer, of love, of lasting joy for your life, in the name of the Father, the Son, and the Holy Spirit.

Baby dearest,
you are the sunshine in my life.
I thank God for your
smile and sweet dependence on me.
Although you need me so much,
I need you even more—
it's amazing how your presence
in a room can always change
my mood for the brighter.
I love you, little one.

God is always near me,

Hearing what I say;
Knowing all my thoughts and deeds,
All my work and play.

God is always near me,
In the darkest night,
He can see me just the same
As by midday light.

God is always near me,
Though so young and small;
Not a look, or word, or thought,
But God knows it all.

PHILIP PAUL BLISS

Every child is God's miracle.

PHILIP BAILEY

Father asked us what was God's noblest work. Anna said men, but I said babies. Men are often bad, but babies never are.

LOUISA MAY ALCOTT

Sources

Brownlow, Leroy, *A Psalm in My Heart,* (Fort Worth, Texas: Brownlow Publishing Company, 1995).

Fant, Gene & Lisa, *Expectant Moments,* © 1999 by Gene and Lisa Fant, (Grand Rapids, MI: ZondervanPublishingHouse, 1999).

Kopp, David and Heather, Reprinted from *Praying the Bible for Your Children.* Copyright ©1997 by David and Heather Kopp. Used by permission of Waterbrook Press, Colorado Springs, Co. All rights reserved.

Sprinkle, Patricia H., *A Gift from God,* Previously published as *In God's Image,* © 1988, 1994 by Patricia H. Sprinkle, (Grand Rapids, MI: ZondervanPublishingHouse, 1994).

Ward, Brenda & John, *For This Child I Pray,* (Fort Worth, Texas: Brownlow Publishing Company, 2000).

Weedn, Flavia & Lisa, *Blessings of Motherhood,* (San Rafael, CA: Cedco Publishing Company, 1999).

Wells, Robert G., Ken Gire, Mary C. Wells and Judy Gire, *Miracle of Life,* © 1993 by Robert G. Wells and Ken Gire, (Grand Rapids, MI: ZondervanPublishingHouse, 1993).

She Calls Me Daddy by Robert D. Wolgemuth, a Focus on the Family book published by Tyndale House. Copyright ©1996 by Robert D. Wolgemuth. All rights reserved. International copyright secured. Used by permission.